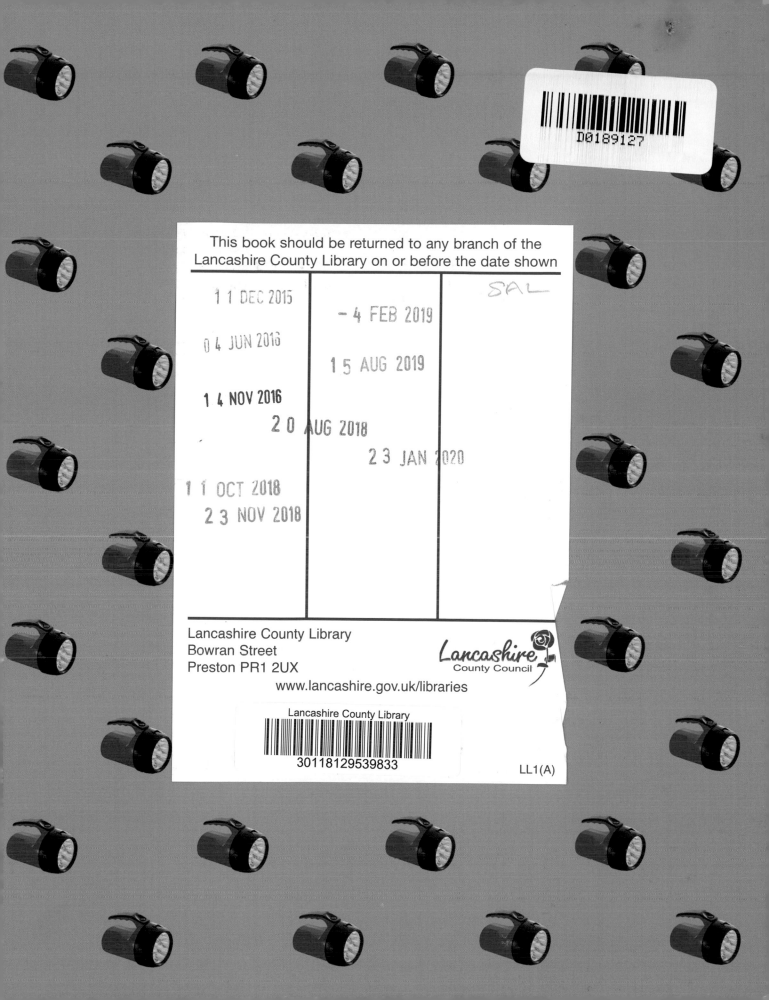

D0189127

This book should be returned to any branch of the
Lancashire County Library on or before the date shown

1 1 DEC 2015

0 4 JUN 2016

1 4 NOV 2016

1 1 OCT 2018
2 3 NOV 2018

- 4 FEB 2019

1 5 AUG 2019

2 0 AUG 2018

2 3 JAN 2020

SAL

Lancashire County Library
Bowran Street
Preston PR1 2UX
www.lancashire.gov.uk/libraries

Lancashire
County Council

Lancashire County Library

30118129539833

LL1(A)

one-stop
science

Experiments
with a
Torch

By Angela Royston

W
FRANKLIN WATTS
LONDON·SYDNEY

This edition 2014
by Franklin Watts

Copyright © Franklin Watts 2011

Franklin Watts
338 Euston Road
London NW1 3BH

Franklin Watts Australia
Level 17/207 Kent Street
Sydney, NSW 2000

All rights reserved.

Series editor: Sarah Peutrill
Art director: Jonathan Hair
Design: Matt Lilly and Ruth Walton
Science consultant: Meredith Blakeney
Photographs: Paul Bricknell, unless
otherwise credited
Models: Rianna Aniakor, Yusuf Hofri, Samuel
Knudsen, India May Nugent, Lyia Sheikh

Credits: Ashley Cooper/Alamy: 6b. Marc
Dietrich/Shutterstock: 7c. Artem
Illarionov/Shutterstock: 7cl. Tom King/Alamy: 7t.
Kokhanchikov/Shutterstock: 11b.
LampLighterSDV/Shutterstock: 19b. Matt Lilly: 23b,
25b. magicinfoto/Shutterstock: 21b.
moodboard/Alamy: 6c. Shaun Robinson/
Shutterstock: 27b. Pedro Salaverria/
Shutterstock: 8c. Kippy Spilker/Shutterstock: 17b.
Tuna Tirkaz/istockphoto: 6t. Alaettin
Yildirm/Shutterstock: 7cr. Every attempt has been
made to clear copyright. Should there be any
inadvertent omission please apply to the publisher
for rectification.

Dewey number: 535'.078
pb ISBN: 978 1 4451 2978 5
Library ebook ISBN: 978 1 4451 2209 0

Printed in China

Franklin Watts is a division of Hachette
Children's Books, an Hachette UK company.
www.hachette.co.uk

Lancashire Library Services

30118129539833

PETERS	J535ROY
£8.99	22-Aug-2014
SAL	

Contents

Words in **bold** are in the glossary on page 28.

What is a torch?

A torch is a **device** that makes light. It contains **batteries** that produce **electricity** to light up the **bulb**. Torches are small and lightweight and so are easy to carry around.

Torches are particularly useful for seeing outdoors at night. Campers use them in their tents and around the campsite. Security guards and the police use them to search dark and shadowy places.

◀ A torch gives a single beam of light. Some torches give a stronger light than other torches.

Kinds of torch

Torches are different shapes, depending on how they are used. A headlamp is a torch that is fixed to a headband. It points exactly where you are looking and leaves both of your hands free for doing other things. **Pot-holers**, for example, use headlamps to explore caves and tunnels underground.

▲ Pot-holers often have to crawl along narrow, dark tunnels. A headlamp is the best kind of torch to light their way.

On your bike

Cycle lamps are a kind of torch, too. Cyclists should have cycle lamps fitted to the front and back of their bicycles. Some cycle lamps flash on and off so that the drivers of motor vehicles can see them more easily.

◀ When it is dark, cycle lamps help other people to see the cyclist.

LED torches

Most torches use a bulb that is a smaller version of a traditional light bulb. An LED torch uses a light emitting diode, which gives a brighter light than a traditional bulb. It also uses less energy, which means that the batteries last longer.

▲ Torches vary in size as well as shape. Bigger torches use more powerful batteries than smaller torches.

The experiments in this book use a torch to explore light and shadows, and other aspects of science including electricity. They will work best in a dimly lit room, using a powerful torch that gives a strong light.

Taking a torch apart

All torches need electricity to work. Most have batteries that produce the electricity, but the batteries have to be in the correct position for the electricity to flow.

You will need:
A torch that works

1 Find out how to turn the torch on and off. Take out the batteries and examine them. Each one has a plus and a minus sign.

2 Put the batteries back in the torch and turn it on. Try turning each battery first one way round and then the other. Make a note of the positions of the plus and minus ends each time. How many ways can you get the torch to work?

What happened?

The bulb lit up when electricity travelled from the batteries through the torch and bulb and back to the batteries. Electricity needs an unbroken path, called a circuit, to flow through. The circuit is only completed when the plus end of one battery is connected to the minus end of the other battery.

Make your own circuit

You will need:
2 pieces of copper wire
about 15 cm long
An AA battery
Sticky tape
A torch bulb

1 Stick a piece of copper wire to each end of the battery.

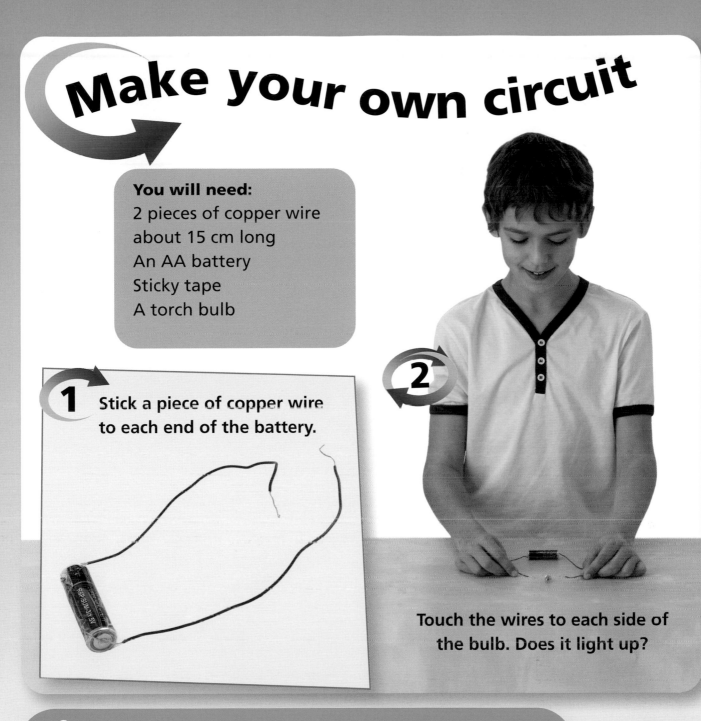

2

Touch the wires to each side of the bulb. Does it light up?

What happened?

When the wires touched the bulb, they completed the circuit. Electricity from the battery flowed through the bulb and lit it up. Electricity always flows in the same direction, from the plus end of the battery to the minus end.

Light travels in straight lines

Light does not bend around shapes like sound does. Light always travels in a straight line. This torch experiment proves it!

You will need:
A torch
3 postcards
A piece of A4 paper
A large nail
Modelling clay
Black card
Paper, pencil and ruler

1

Hold the postcards so that the bottom edges are on top of each other. Make a hole through the middle using the nail.

2 Draw a pencil line down the centre of the paper. Lay three small lumps of clay along the pencil line about 3 cm apart.

3

Place the black card in the furthest piece of clay. Place a postcard in each of the other two pieces so that the hole in the postcard is above the line on the paper.

4 Shine the torch through the hole in the first postcard. Tilt the torch slightly until the circle of light hits the hole in the second postcard. Can you see the light on the black card? Turn the torch a little to the left. What happens?

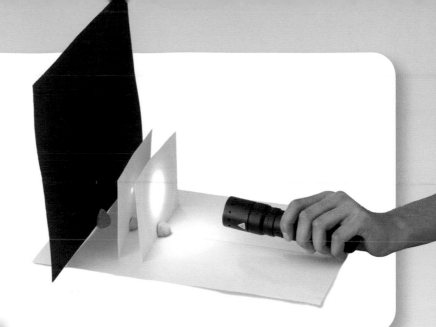

5 Add the third card in front of the other cards. Can you still get the beam to hit the black card?

6 Take away the postcard nearest the black card. Now take away the next postcard. What happens to the spot of light?

What happened?

When the holes were lined up in a straight line, the beam travelled straight through them. The bigger the gap between the last hole and the black screen, the larger the final circle of light. This is because the light spreads out.

◄ The light from this old film projector spreads out to fill the screen.

Making shadows

When light hits an object a **shadow** forms behind it. Find out what different shadows you can make with various objects, including your hands.

You will need:
A torch
A mug
Building blocks
A white wall or screen
A transparent plastic bottle

 1 Hold the mug about 4 cm from the wall or screen, and shine the torch on it. What shape is the shadow?

2 Do you think that something that is transparent will create a shadow? Shine the torch onto the plastic bottle and see if you are right.

3 Make a stack of blocks. Shine the torch onto the stack. What happens to the shadow when you change the arrangement of the stack?

What happened?

When light hits an object, some of the light is blocked but the rest travels on in straight lines past the object. So the space behind the object is less well lit than the space around it. This forms a shadow that is exactly the same shape as the object.

Making shapes

Use your hands to make these shapes. Ask a friend to shine the torch on your hands to make the shadows. What shapes are the shadows? What other shapes can you make?

Exploring shadows

Find out how the position of an object can change the size and shape of its shadow.

You will need:
A torch
An object, such as a small plastic figure
A table
A white wall or screen
Ruler, paper and pencil

1 Place the figure on the table 10 cm from the screen. Place the torch on the table 30 cm from the screen and shine it on the figure. Measure the height of the shadow and write it down.

2 Now move the figure so that it is 15 cm from the screen. Measure the height of the shadow again. Repeat with the figure 20 cm from the screen.

3 Make a graph to show how the size of the shadow changes as the figure is moved away from the screen.

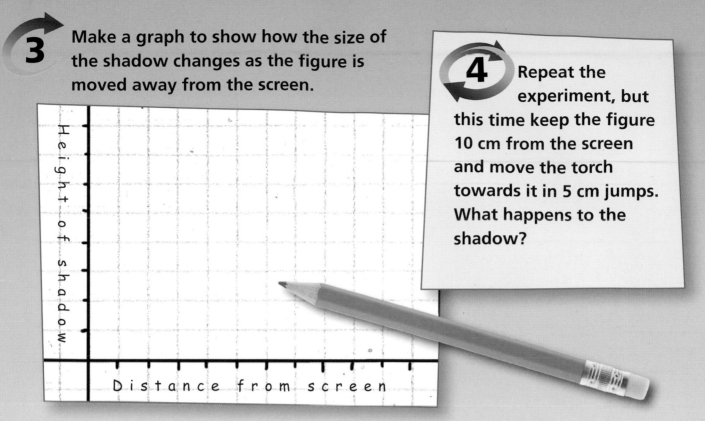

Height of shadow

Distance from screen

4 Repeat the experiment, but this time keep the figure 10 cm from the screen and move the torch towards it in 5 cm jumps. What happens to the shadow?

Changing shape

Keep the figure on the table but change the height of the torch. Start with the torch 30 cm behind the figure and 30 cm above the table. Slowly lower the torch but keep it shining on the figure. What happens to the shadow?

The Sun

The height of the Sun in the sky changes during the day. Measure the height and direction of the shadow of a stick (stuck upright in the ground) at different times during the day. How do you think sundials work?

Bouncing light

When light hits an object, some of it bounces off. Some surfaces **reflect** light better than others. This experiment will work best in a dark or dim room.

You will need:
A torch
A mirror

1 Shine the torch into the mirror and look for the reflection of the light on the wall. Where do you think the reflected light will be if you angle the torch to the left?

2 Angle the torch to the left. Was your prediction correct? Now predict where the light will be when you angle the beam to the right, then up and then down. Test your predictions.

What happened?

Light travels in straight lines, so, when it hit the mirror at an angle, it was reflected at an angle. Light is only reflected straight back to you when you point it straight at the mirror.

Testing other surfaces

Collect some shiny objects such as a shiny, flat top, a tin of food, a piece of metal foil, and a mirror. Shine the torch on each object. Which reflects light the best? Which one shines the least?

Reflectors

Reflector strips, like those used on safety jackets, help to make people easier to see at night. Reflector strips use glass beads which work like tiny mirrors to reflect car lights and other lights.

◀ Firefighters wear clothes with reflective strips so that they can be seen in the dark.

Making light bend

Light always travels in straight lines – or does it? This torch experiment works best in a dimly lit or dark room.

You will need:
A torch
A small, clear plastic bottle
Metal foil
A coloured plastic bowl
A jug of water

1 Wrap the metal foil around the side of the bottle. Make sure the top and bottom are not covered.

2 Fill the bottle with water. Press the torch against the bottom of the bottle and switch it on.

Hold the torch firmly against the bottle as you slowly pour the water into the bowl. Can you see a patch of light at the bottom of the bowl? Look closely at the water flowing between the bottle and the bowl. Can you see the beam of light bending with the water?

What happened?

The light looks as if it is bending, but it is being reflected from side to side inside the stream of water.

Fibre optics

This experiment shows how fibre optics works. An optical fibre is a narrow glass tube that carries signals in the form of light. It is used, for example, to carry telephone signals and works much better than the traditional method of passing electrical signals along a metal wire.

▶ Each of these fibre optic cables can carry up to 10 million signals at the same time.

Making coloured lights

This experiment shows you how to make different coloured lights and explores how colour **filters** work.

You will need:
A torch
3 clear, square plastic water bottles, about a third filled with water
Red, blue and green food dyes
A sheet of white paper

1 Add a few drops of red dye to the first bottle.

2 Hold the paper behind the bottle and shine the torch through the coloured water. What colour is the patch of light?

3 Add a few drops of blue dye to the second bottle and a few drops of green dye to the third bottle. What colour do you think the light patch will be for each? Were you right?

4 Put the red water in front of the blue water. What colour do you think the patch will be now? Were you right? What happens with different combinations of coloured water?

Filters that are pure red, blue and green give the best results. Food dyes have other colours mixed with them, so they may not cut out the light completely.

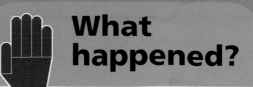

What happened?

The red water acted as a red filter, which allowed only red light to pass through it. Similarly the blue filter allowed only blue light through and the green filter allowed only green light to pass through. So when you shone the light through two different coloured filters, no light reached the paper!

Filters on stage
Colour filters are used by lighting experts to create exciting effects on stage for concerts and plays.

Mixing coloured lights

When you mix red and blue paints you get purple. What happens when you mix red and blue lights?

You will need:
3 identical torches
Red, blue and green filters
Sticky tape
White paper

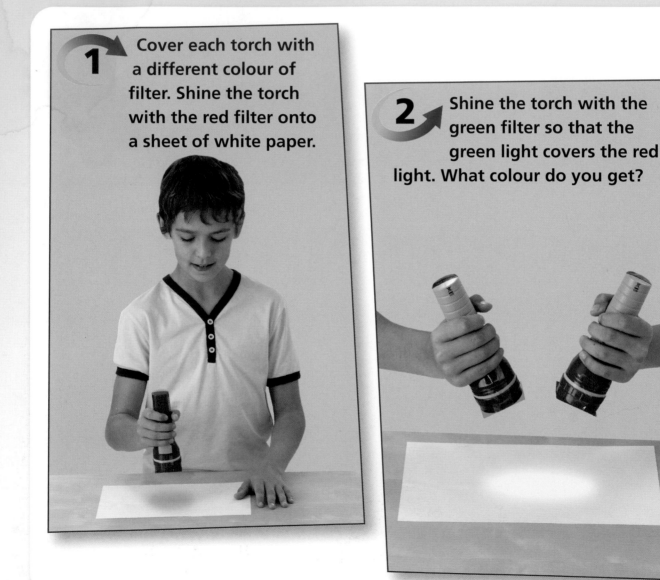

1 Cover each torch with a different colour of filter. Shine the torch with the red filter onto a sheet of white paper.

2 Shine the torch with the green filter so that the green light covers the red light. What colour do you get?

3 Now shine the torch with the blue filter so that its light falls on top of the other two colours. Ask a friend to help you if you need to. What colour of light do you get now?

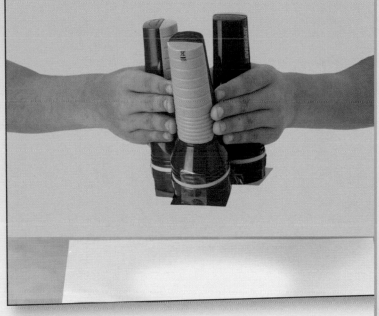

What happened?

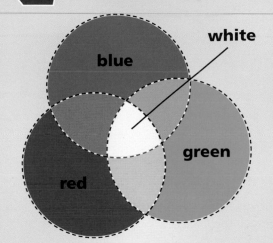

blue
white
green
red

When you shone the green light onto the red light, you should have seen an orange-yellow light. When you shone the blue light on top of it, you should have got white light. White light is made up of all the different colours of the **spectrum**.

Theatre spotlights

Theatre producers use different coloured **spotlights** to light the stage. Sometimes they mix the colours to make different colours.

Make a rainbow

In this experiment you will split white light up so that you can see the different colours, as in a rainbow.

You will need:
A torch
A circle of black card to cover the face of the torch
Sticky tape and scissors
A mirror
A plastic box
White card
Modelling clay
Jug of water

1 Cut the circle of black card in half. Stick each half over the front of the torch leaving a narrow slit between the two halves.

2 Pour water into the plastic box until the water is about 2.5 cm deep.

3 Place the mirror in the box so that it is slanted and covered by the water. Hold the mirror in place with modelling clay.

4 Shine the torch onto the mirror through the water.

5 Catch the reflection on the white card. Adjust the angle of the mirror and the torch until you can see the different colours in the reflection on the paper.

What happened?

Different colours of light travel through water at different speeds. This split the light up into the colours of the spectrum. The colours are always in the same order: red, orange, yellow, green, blue, violet. One colour merges into the next one.

Rainbows

A rainbow is made when sunlight shines through drops of water. The drops split the light into the separate colours. The biggest rainbows form in the sky, but you may see a rainbow when the Sun shines through water from a sprinkler hose.

What makes the sky turn red?

In broad daylight the sky is blue, except when it is cloudy. When the Sun sets and rises, however, the sky looks pink. This experiment produces the same result.

You will need:
A torch
A transparent plastic box
Water
Milk

1 Fill the box with water.

2 Now add a small amount of milk so that the water turns slightly cloudy. You have added white milk to clear water, but what colour is the liquid?

3 Place the torch at one end of the box and shine it through the liquid.

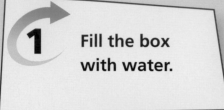

Look at the liquid from the other end of the box. What colour is it?

4 Look at the box from the side or from above. Can you see the colour change gradually from blue to orange-red?

What happened?

As the beam of light hit small particles of milk, the light broke up into different colours. Blue light is easily scattered, so this is the colour you see first. The remaining colours combined to give an orange-red light, which carried on to the end of the box.

Sunrise and sunset

The sky looks pink or red at sunrise and sunset. This is because the Sun's rays pass through air that is close to the ground where there are more particles to scatter the light. By the time the light reaches you, most of the blue light has been scattered by the particles, leaving the reddish light.

Glossary

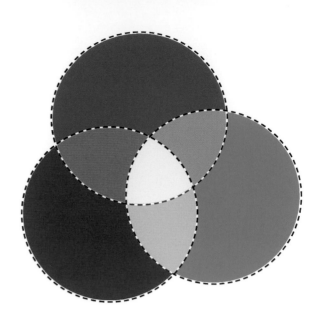

battery something that contains chemicals that react to generate electricity.

bulb a glass globe that produces electric light.

device something designed for a particular purpose.

electricity a form of energy which can be used to produce light, heat, motion and other things.

filter a device that allows part of something to pass through it, but blocks the rest of it. A coloured filter allows only light of that colour to pass through it.

pot-holer someone who explores tunnels and caves deep underground.

reflect bounce light back.

reflector something that reflects light.

shadow an area that is less well lit than the surrounding area. A shadow is produced when a beam of light is blocked by an object.

spectrum the band of colours that together make up white light.

spotlight a lamp that shines a strong beam of light on a small area.

Further information

Websites

www.bbc.co.uk/schools/scienceclips/ages/7_8/science_7_8.shtml
Click on 'Light and shadows' to get an interactive experiment with shadows.

www.exploratorium.edu/snacks/iconlight.html
Gives a list of experiments exploring different aspects of light.

www.opticalres.com/kidoptx_f.html
A website produced by Optical Research Associates that includes interactive ways of exploring light, lenses and lasers.

www.sciencemuseum.org.uk/educators/classroom_and_homework_resources/ks2/light.aspx
The Science Museum extends the ideas of Launchpad into the classroom and includes activities for making a periscope and coloured shadows that recombine to give 3D glasses.

Note to parents and teachers: Every effort has been made by the Publishers to ensure that these websites are suitable for children, that they are of the highest educational value, and that they contain no inappropriate or offensive material. However, because of the nature of the Internet, it is impossible to guarantee that the contents of these sites will not be altered. We strongly advise that Internet access is supervised by a responsible adult.

Books

The Real Scientist: Flash! Light and How We See Things
by Peter Riley (Franklin Watts, 2012)

Amazing Science: Light by Sally Hewitt
(Wayland, 2014)

Index

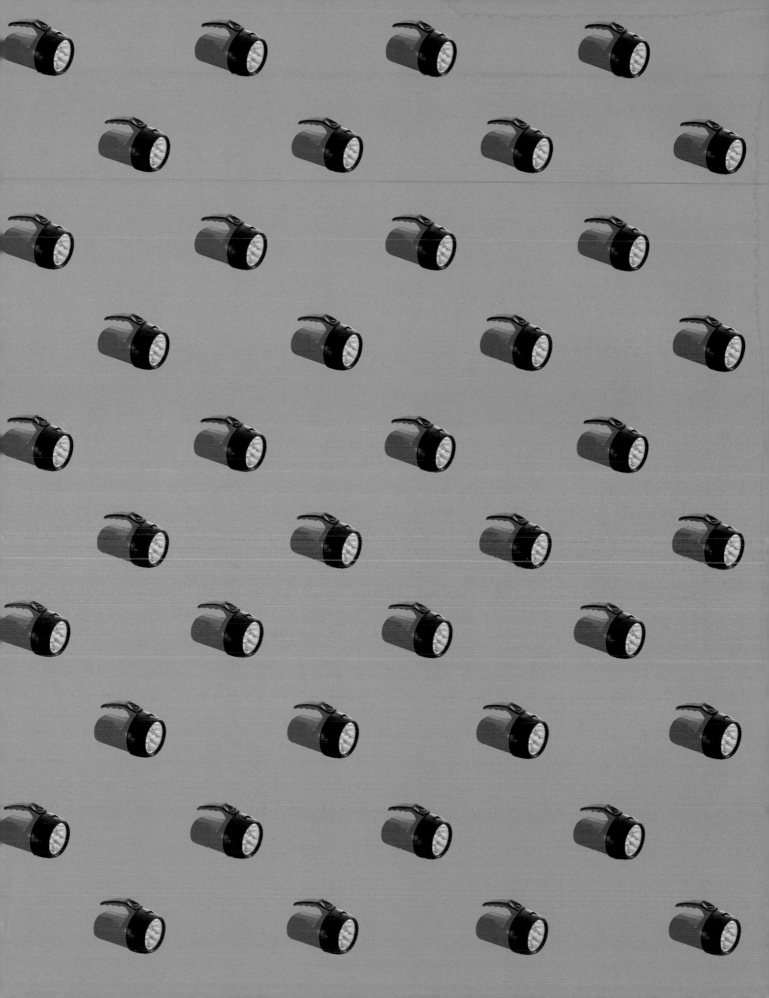